INSIDE THE NBA

LOS ANGELES CLIPPERS

BY PATRICK DONNELLY

SportsZone

An Imprint of Abdo Publishing
abdobooks.com

abdobooks.com

Published by Abdo Publishing, a division of ABDO, PO Box 398166, Minneapolis, Minnesota 55439. Copyright © 2023 by Abdo Consulting Group, Inc. International copyrights reserved in all countries. No part of this book may be reproduced in any form without written permission from the publisher. SportsZone™ is a trademark and logo of Abdo Publishing.

Printed in China.
052022
092022

Cover Photo: Douglas P. DeFelice/Getty Images Sport/Getty Images
Interior Photos: Melinda Nagy/Shutterstock Images, 1; Jevone Moore/Icon Sportswire/Getty Images, 4; Sean M. Haffey/Getty Images Sport/Getty Images, 7; Kevork Djansezian/Getty Images Sport/Getty Images, 9, 10; George Gojkovich/Getty Images Sport/Getty Images, 12; Focus on Sport/Getty Images, 14, 24, 34; Focus on Sport/Getty Images Sport/Getty Images, 17; Mike Powell/Allsport/Getty Images Sport/Getty Images, 18; Christian Petersen/Getty Images Sport/Getty Images, 20; Marcio Jose Sanchez/AP Images, 23; Kirby Lee/AP Images, 27; Mark Ralston/AFP/Getty Images, 29; Chris Chambers/Getty Images Sport/Getty Images, 31; Soobum Im/Getty Images Sport/Getty Images, 32; Lisa Blumenfeld/Getty Images Sport/Getty Images, 37, 38; Ashley Landis/AP Images, 41

Editor: Charlie Beattie
Series Designer: Joshua Olson

Library of Congress Control Number: 2021951655

Publisher's Cataloging-in-Publication Data

Names: Donnelly, Patrick, author.
Title: Los Angeles Clippers / by Patrick Donnelly
Description: Minneapolis, Minnesota: Abdo Publishing, 2023 | Series: Inside the NBA | Includes online resources and index.
Identifiers: ISBN 9781532198304 (lib. bdg.) | ISBN 9781098271954 (ebook)
Subjects: LCSH: Los Angeles Clippers (Basketball team)--Juvenile literature. | Basketball--Juvenile literature. | Professional sports--Juvenile literature. | Sports franchises--Juvenile literature.
Classification: DDC 796.32364--dc23

TABLE OF CONTENTS

CHAPTER ONE

COMEBACK KIDS

he Los Angeles Clippers had dug themselves quite a hole. It was still early in the third quarter. But the Clippers trailed the Utah Jazz by 25 points in Game 6 of the 2021 Western Conference semifinals. Los Angeles entered the game leading the Jazz 3–2. One more victory would send the Clippers to the conference finals for the first time in the team's 51-year history. And the game was being played in Los Angeles. Los Angeles hoped to wrap up the series and avoid a trip back to Utah for a winner-take-all Game 7. But those hopes were fading by the second.

Being behind didn't faze Paul George. Like the Clippers franchise, its star small forward had endured plenty of frustrations in his career. He'd experienced devastating playoff losses and even worse injuries. George had come too far to give up.

Clippers forward Paul George averaged 26.9 points, 9.6 rebounds, and 5.4 assists during the team's 2021 playoff run.

Utah led 75–50 when George scored on a dunk off a Jazz turnover. It didn't seem all that significant at the time, but it was the start of a historic comeback for Los Angeles.

THE NEW CLIPPERS

There was a time when the Clippers hadn't dreamed of playing in games like this. For most of its time in Los Angeles, the team had been the laughingstock of the National Basketball Association (NBA). The Clippers had arrived in California's most glamorous city in 1984. It took them 21 more years just to win a playoff series.

This was a new era of Clippers basketball. In the 2010s, the team had become a consistent contender. Los Angeles played exciting basketball. Star players, who once fled the Clippers as soon as they got the chance, signed up to play.

That was certainly true in the summer of 2019. Two established stars came on board. George had been one of the NBA's best forwards during his time with the Indiana Pacers and Oklahoma City Thunder. Another forward, Kawhi Leonard, was even more accomplished. Leonard was a two-time NBA champion. Both times he was Most Valuable Player (MVP) of the NBA Finals. He had also won the NBA's Defensive Player of the Year award twice. The arrival of both players put Los Angeles in the NBA title conversation.

George, *left*, and forward Kawhi Leonard, *right*, turned the Clippers into one of the NBA's most exciting teams when they joined up in the summer of 2019.

However, heading into Game 6, one of the Clippers' stars was missing. Leonard had injured his knee in Game 4. He had not played since. George faced the prospect of turning the tide against Utah all on his own, unless other players stepped up.

CLIMBING THE HILL

A few minutes after his steal and dunk, George picked up another steal. He passed ahead to Clippers guard Terance Mann, who was racing down the sideline at midcourt. Mann met up with two Jazz players defending the rim. But he found enough space to lay it in. The Clippers had scored nine straight points to cut Utah's lead to 75–59. Sensing trouble, Jazz coach Quin Snyder called timeout.

It worked, at least for a while. Utah's lead swelled to 21 points again with 6:37 left in the third. But the Clippers weren't out yet. Mann and guard Reggie Jackson started a huge Los Angeles push. Over the next 5:05, the pair combined for 19 points. George chipped in a pair of free throws. Meanwhile, Utah's shots were clanking off the iron. When Jackson hit a three-pointer with 1:42 left, the Clippers trailed by only two.

By now, the crowd of more than 17,000 fans at Staples Center was roaring. The fans were used to seeing the home team collapse when the going got tough. The Clippers had reached the conference semifinals four times in the previous nine seasons. Each time, they failed to advance. Perhaps this was the team to end that streak.

PUTTING IT AWAY

Utah took a 94–91 lead into the fourth quarter. But Clippers forward Nicolas Batum tied it with a three-pointer in the first

Clippers guards Reggie Jackson, *right*, and Terrance Mann acknowledge the crowd during the second half of Game 6 against the Utah Jazz.

minute. Jackson then drove for a layup that put the Clippers ahead. And the onslaught continued. Even guard Patrick Beverley, better known for his defense, hit a three from the corner. George sank a three from the same spot. Jackson drove for another bucket, and Batum hit another three-pointer. The Clippers led 107–100 with just under nine minutes remaining.

Utah made one last push. The Jazz scored the next six points. But the Clippers were rolling. Los Angeles had roasted Utah's defense for 41 points in the third quarter. The Clippers

Second-year guard Mann, *left*, had scored more than 20 points only four times in his career before pouring in 39 against the Jazz.

were on that pace again. George and Mann quickly piled up a 9–0 run.

Utah had run out of answers. The Jazz never moved closer than four points the rest of the way. The final score was 131–119. The Clippers outscored the Jazz 81–47 in the second half. It was the biggest comeback by a team in a playoff series–clinching win in 25 years.

Even without Leonard, the Clippers had come through. Other players had stepped up. Before this, Mann had never scored more than 25 points in any game. In fact, he had scored 25 total points in the first five games of the series. But in Game 6, the second-year forward exploded for 39 points. George added 28. Jackson scored 27 and added 10 assists.

When the final buzzer sounded, the Clippers embraced. They congratulated the Jazz on a hard-fought series. The fans continued to cheer. But they had to wonder if what they had just seen had really happened. The Clippers were in the conference finals for the first time.

"It was just a special night. You know, you felt it, the cheers, the excitement. The playoffs are about grit. It's about fighting. It's about whatever it takes, and time after time, I think we've shown that."

BRAVES
8

CHAPTER TWO

LONG ROAD TO LA

The NBA went through a period of change in the 1960s. The league finished the 1965–66 season with nine teams. But the popularity of professional basketball was growing. A rival league launched in 1967. It was called the American Basketball Association (ABA). The ABA was eager to bring the sport to cities that the NBA had ignored for years.

The NBA wanted to get ahead of its new rival. The league placed teams into many of those markets before the ABA could. By the time the 1970–71 season began, the NBA had nearly doubled in size. Eight new teams had joined the league.

One of those new teams was the Buffalo Braves. Buffalo, New York, didn't have much of a basketball history. The city had a team for a very short time in 1946. That was before the NBA existed. The Buffalo Bisons played in the National Basketball League. But the team played just 13 games before

Buffalo Braves forward Marvin Barnes (8) battles for a rebound against the Los Angeles Lakers in 1978.

Head coach Jack Ramsay led Buffalo to three straight playoff appearances in the 1970s.

the owners moved them out of town.

The Braves joined the NBA in 1970 along with the Cleveland Cavaliers and the Portland Trail Blazers. Like most expansion teams, Buffalo struggled early on. Their roster was filled with rookies and castoffs from the league's more established teams. Buffalo went 22–60 in each of its first two seasons.

The team also had off-court struggles. The first owners ran into money problems. Local businessman Paul Snyder stepped in and purchased the team. But Snyder had a tough problem to solve. The Braves shared an arena with two other teams. A local school, Canisius College, also used the Buffalo's Memorial Auditorium for basketball. Buffalo's professional hockey team, the Sabres, did too. Finding dates to play home games was tough for the Braves. The situation got so bad that the Braves played some of their home games in nearby Syracuse and Rochester. They also crossed the border and played in Toronto, Canada.

MAKING STRIDES

Buffalo took a big step forward in 1972 when they hired former Philadelphia 76ers head coach Jack Ramsay. They also drafted star center Bob McAdoo. He went on to lead the NBA in scoring three straight years. In the 1973–74 season, the team posted its first winning record at 42–40. That was good enough to reach the playoffs for the first time. Buffalo returned to the playoffs in each of the next two seasons as well.

The highlight of the team's tenure in Buffalo came in 1975–76. They won 46 games and knocked off the 76ers in the first round of the playoffs. But the good times didn't last. Ramsay left for Portland, where he led the Trail Blazers to the NBA title in his first season. McAdoo and other top players were traded.

Super Swap

The Buffalo Braves were key players in the biggest trade in NBA history. But they didn't swap a handful of superstars with another team. In 1978 Buffalo's new ownership traded the entire franchise. Irving Levin owned the Boston Celtics. He wanted to move them to the West Coast. But the league wouldn't consider relocating one of its premier teams. Instead, Levin traded franchises with Buffalo's new owners. Levin immediately moved his new team to San Diego and named them the Clippers.

The Braves' win totals dropped to 30 and then 27 the next
two seasons.

And then they were gone. Snyder had sold the team, and
the new owners didn't want to keep the team in Buffalo. In
1978 the team was sold again. The Braves moved across the
country. The next year they settled into their new home in San
Diego, California.

NO FUN IN THE SUN

San Diego had already struck out once as an NBA market. The
expansion San Diego Rockets were founded in 1967. Four years
later, the team moved to Houston, Texas. An ABA team later
came and went as well. But the NBA decided to give San Diego
another chance. A contest was held to name the new team.
"Clippers" was chosen because of the clipper ships often seen
in the water outside the city.

The move looked promising at first. The Clippers won 43
games in their first season behind high-scoring guard World
B. Free. But that wasn't good enough to reach the playoffs
in the tough Western Conference. Unfortunately, that was as
good as it got in San Diego. Injuries to star players, including
center Bill Walton, and unsuccessful trades took their tolls. The
team fell to a record of 17–65 in 1981–82. Attendance dropped
significantly. New owner Donald Sterling began cutting corners

Because of injuries, Bill Walton played only 169 of a possible 492 games during his six seasons with the San Diego/Los Angeles Clippers.

to save money. The Clippers became one of the worst teams in the league year after year.

LA-LA LAND

Up the coast in Los Angeles, basketball was thriving. The Los Angeles Lakers had a dynasty in the 1980s. Sterling wanted to move his new team there too. But the NBA said no when he

Danny Manning made two All-Star teams in six seasons with the Clippers.

brought up the idea in 1982. Two years later, Sterling decided he'd move the team anyway. The decision angered the league. The NBA fined Sterling $25 million. It also wanted to force Sterling and the Clippers back to San Diego.

Sterling sued the NBA. When it looked as if he might win, the league backed down. The Clippers were allowed to stay, and the fine was reduced to $6 million.

The lawsuit was about the only win for the team in that era. The Clippers brought their history of losing with them. In their first seven years in Los Angeles, they had never won more than 32 games. That included a 12–70 record in 1986–87. It was one of the worst seasons by any team in NBA history.

There were many reasons for the Clippers' struggles. Sterling still refused to spend money. The team had trouble attracting quality free agents. Several high draft picks also turned out to be busts.

When the Clippers finally did pick the right man, injuries came back to haunt them again. University of Kansas forward Danny Manning had led the Jayhawks to the national title in 1988. He had been a college All-American twice, among other awards. The Clippers made him the first pick of that summer's NBA Draft.

Before he could repeat his college success in the pros, Manning was hurt. He suffered a torn knee ligament just 26 games into his rookie year. He missed the rest of the season. Manning was never the same again.

Manning's absence had one silver lining, however. The Clippers played poorly enough to land the number two pick in the 1989 draft. They used it on former Duke University forward

Led by stars like DeAndre Jordan (6) and Chris Paul (3), the Clippers became one of the NBA's most exciting teams in the 2010s.

Danny Ferry. But by now the Clippers, and Sterling, had a bad reputation. Ferry decided he didn't want to play for the team. He spent the year in Italy instead. The Clippers traded him to the Cleveland Cavaliers.

THE BREAKTHROUGH

In 1990–91 the Clippers posted their tenth straight season of at least 50 losses. But the team put together two playoff appearances in a row the next two years. Manning was back playing regularly. And the team had a star guard in Ron Harper. Despite back-to-back first-round playoff losses, Clippers fans were hopeful their luck was turning.

Instead, the team collapsed again. The Clippers made the playoffs just once in the next 12 years. Even that appearance was misleading. In 1996–97 the Western Conference was weak. The Clippers snuck into the postseason despite winning only 36 games. They were quickly swept by the Utah Jazz.

Things finally started to change in 2005–06. The Clippers' improvement was fueled by another big man from Duke, forward Elton Brand. He led the team to not only the postseason but also a series victory. The Clippers knocked off the Denver Nuggets in five games for their first playoff win since 1976, back when the team was still in Buffalo.

In typical Clippers fashion, however, the team couldn't keep moving forward. Another five-year playoff drought followed.

LOB CITY

Despite struggling, the Clippers were getting better at finding talent. In the 2008 draft, they landed guard Eric Gordon in the first round. Center DeAndre Jordan was picked in the second round. The next year they selected forward Blake Griffin first overall. In December 2011 general manager Neil Olshey brought in superstar guard Chris Paul via a trade.

Griffin, Paul, and Jordan formed a solid team core. The group made the playoffs for six straight seasons. Even better, they were among the NBA's most exciting teams. Griffin and Jordan were both thunderous dunkers. And with Paul tossing them passes, the team earned a catchy nickname—"Lob City." NBA fans flocked to see highlights of the new Clippers.

Paul moved on after the 2016–17 season, and Griffin and Jordan were gone a year later. But the Clippers had developed a taste for winning. And NBA free agents finally saw the Clippers as an attractive option. That was particularly true after the much-hated Sterling was stripped of team ownership in 2014. He had been recorded making racist statements. Some of them referenced players on his own team. The Clippers were eventually taken over by businessman Steve Ballmer.

In the summer of 2019, two of the biggest names in the NBA joined forces for the Clippers. Forward Kawhi Leonard had just led the Toronto Raptors to the NBA title. Fellow forward Paul George was coming off his fourth straight All-Star season.

Kawhi Leonard (2) averaged a career-high 27.1 points per game during his first season with the Clippers in 2019–20.

They led the Clippers to back-to-back playoff appearances. That included a spot in the 2021 Western Conference finals. After decades of misery, the Clippers had finally shaken the label of NBA laughingstock.

CHAPTER THREE

CLIPPER CAPTAINS

Bob McAdoo's first professional game was typical of his first season with the Buffalo Braves. He scored 20 points and grabbed 10 rebounds. And the struggling Braves lost by 11 to the Atlanta Hawks.

McAdoo came to the team in 1972 after one dominant college season at the University of North Carolina. Individual accomplishments kept adding up during his four-plus years in Buffalo. In 1973 he won the Rookie of the Year Award. Then he won the next three NBA scoring titles. He averaged more than 30 points a game in each of those seasons. McAdoo's peak came in 1974–75, when he scored 34.5 points per game. For that performance, he added the NBA MVP Award.

Standing 6 feet, 9 inches and weighing 210 pounds, McAdoo caused matchup problems for defenses. He was too big for most forwards to guard him, but he was too quick for

Buffalo's playoff teams of the 1970s were built around high-scoring forward Bob McAdoo, *center*.

most centers. In an era when most big men still played down low with their backs to the basket, McAdoo's shooting touch made him a threat from the outside as well.

After that rough first season, McAdoo led Buffalo to three straight playoff appearances before the team traded him to the Knicks in December 1976 to save money. He ended up playing for seven teams in his Hall-of-Fame career.

DUKE CONNECTION

The Clippers teams of the 1980s and '90s weren't known for their star-studded rosters. That began to change in 2001, when the team acquired center Elton Brand in a trade with the Chicago Bulls. Brand was the first overall pick in the 1999 NBA Draft. He quickly showed that his skills translated to the pro game, winning the Rookie of the Year Award after posting 20.1 points and 10.0 rebounds per game for Chicago.

He didn't miss a beat with the Clippers. He was one of the most consistent scorers and rebounders of his era. In seven seasons with Los Angeles, Brand averaged 20.3 points and 10.3 rebounds per game and was a two-time All-Star. But he needed help to make the Clippers a winning team. In 2005–06 he and another former Duke star, small forward Corey Maggette, paced the team's offense. Veteran point guard Sam Cassell came over in a midseason trade with the Minnesota Timberwolves. The trio led a balanced Clippers roster to its first playoff series win since the team had moved away from Buffalo.

Clippers forward Elton Brand puts up a jump shot against the Dallas Mavericks in 2004.

But Brand and the Clippers couldn't stay in the hunt. The star forward suffered an injured Achilles during a preseason workout and missed all but eight games of the 2007–08 season. He ended up leaving to sign a free-agent contract with the Philadelphia 76ers in July 2008.

LOB CITY STARS

The Clippers chose forward Blake Griffin with the first pick of the 2009 draft. The dynamic leaper came in hyped to turn the franchise around. But like many Clippers draft picks, the injury bug caught Griffin. A broken kneecap sidelined him for what should have been his rookie year. But that didn't stop the 6-foot-9-inch power forward from breaking out in 2010–11. He burst onto the NBA scene by averaging 22.5 points and 12.1 rebounds per game. He was already a fan favorite when he won the dunk contest at the All-Star Game. After the season, he was named Rookie of the Year.

In an age when NBA highlights were quickly turned into viral videos, Griffin was an internet sensation. NBA fans were amazed by the big man's incredible athletic skills.

But Griffin was more than just a dunker. He was an elite rebounder and had a host of solid low-post moves. Injuries started taking their toll on Griffin after his first four seasons in the league. But when he left the team in 2018, Griffin was one of only two players in franchise history with more than 10,000 points.

When Griffin wasn't throwing down slams, center DeAndre Jordan was rattling rims for the Clippers. While Griffin was an instant hit, the 6-foot-11-inch, 265-pound Jordan needed time to become an NBA star. The center was drafted in the second

Blake Griffin hangs on the rim by his elbow during the 2011 All-Star dunk contest.

round of the 2008 draft. For his first five seasons, he never averaged double figures in points or rebounds.

Jordan busted out in 2013–14. That year, he was the NBA's leading rebounder and averaged double figures in scoring for the first time. He repeated both feats the next season. Two years later, Jordan made his first All-Star team. He left the team in 2018 having played 750 games in a Clippers uniform. That was a franchise record.

Jordan's rise to stardom came right after point guard Chris Paul joined the team. Paul was the spark plug the Clippers needed to jump-start their offense when they acquired him before the 2011–12 season. He'd spent his first six seasons with the New Orleans Hornets. There, he'd been named Rookie of the Year and played in four All-Star Games. Paul also led the league in assists twice and steals three times.

In Los Angeles, Paul shored up his reputation as one of the league's best point guards. Once again he was the NBA's top assist man twice. He also led the league in steals three times, just as he had in New Orleans. Paul fed Griffin and Jordan so many perfect alley-oop passes that people around the league began referring to Los Angeles as "Lob City."

Beginning in 2012, the trio led the Clippers to the playoffs six straight seasons. Los Angeles advanced to the second round of the playoffs three times. During that stretch, the

The Clippers made the playoffs for a franchise-record six consecutive seasons after guard Chris Paul arrived in 2011.

Clippers won more playoff series than the franchise's first 41 seasons combined.

NEW FLEET

The Clippers shared a city with the mighty Los Angeles Lakers starting in 1984. The teams had shared an arena since 1999. During that time, the Lakers won multiple NBA championships. The Clippers won nothing. The Lakers signed big-name free agents. Players had historically left the Clippers at the first opportunity.

Paul George made his first All-Star appearance as a Clipper in 2020–21.

However, in 2019 the Clippers were ready to shed the label of Los Angeles's "other" team. Luckily, big names were available that summer as free agents.

First, the Clippers signed the top player on the market, small forward Kawhi Leonard, on July 9. Leonard brought a winning reputation to his new team. He had just won a title with the Toronto Raptors. That was his second championship. He had also won in 2014 with the San Antonio Spurs. Both times, Leonard had been named MVP of the NBA Finals. Early in his career he had been a defensive stopper. But by 2019 Leonard was also a top offensive threat.

The next day, the Clippers made a big trade. Forward Paul George came over in a multiplayer deal with the Oklahoma City Thunder. George was a high-scoring swingman and a regular at the NBA All-Star Game. He was also a top defender. Suddenly the Clippers were looking like a title contender.

They played like it in the pair's first season together. Led by Leonard's 27.1 points per game and George's 21.5, Los Angeles was among the best offenses in the NBA. The wins followed, as the team finished 49–23 and reached the second round of the playoffs.

Leonard and George went back to work the next year, once again filling the stat sheet along the way. And they finally got the Clippers into the Western Conference finals. The run gave Clippers fans hope that perhaps an NBA title might finally be within their grasp.

HIGHLIGHT CLIPS

The Buffalo Braves won just 65 games over their first three seasons. But in 1973–74 they scrapped their way to a 42–40 record. That was good enough for the fourth and final spot in the Eastern Conference playoffs. Once there, Buffalo faced the mighty Boston Celtics.

The series went back and forth, with the home team winning each of the first five games. In the pivotal Game 6, Buffalo center Bob McAdoo scored 40 points and grabbed 15 rebounds. But with the game tied in the final seconds, he fouled Boston guard Jo Jo White.

Buffalo coach Jack Ramsay argued that the foul had occurred after the final buzzer. But the officials disagreed. They gave White two free throws with no time on the clock. White calmly drained both shots, and Boston clinched the series with

Bob McAdoo's stellar play helped Buffalo win its first-ever playoff series in 1976.

a 106–104 victory. The Celtics went on to win their twelfth NBA title.

The next season saw Buffalo fall to the powerful Washington Bullets in the first round. The third time proved to be the charm for the Braves. After a 46-win season in 1975–76, they took on the Philadelphia 76ers in a best-of-three first-round playoff series. The teams split the first two games. But McAdoo proved to be too much for the 76ers in Game 3. He scored 34 points and grabbed 22 rebounds as Buffalo pulled out a 124–123 overtime victory.

BARRY GOES BIG

Clippers guard Brent Barry didn't want to be in the 1996 dunk contest. He could jump out of the gym, but he still wasn't eager to go up against the best dunkers in the world.

"I'd never lost a dunk contest. I don't mean to say that to sound overly confident or cocky. It's the fact that I knew better," Barry said. "I only want to go up against the guys I can beat. I pick

Guard Cuttino Mobley, *left*, forward Elton Brand, *center*, and center Chris Kaman, *right*, helped the Clippers end their playoff drought in 2005–06.

the guys who can't dunk. And then I enter that contest—and win it."

But the struggling Clippers needed some positive attention. They urged Barry to participate. So he showed up at San Antonio's Alamodome on February 10, 1996, hoping to just have a good time.

Performing to a playlist of songs by the rock group Pearl Jam, Barry shocked the arena. He ended his first round with a version of a dunk made famous by Julius Erving and Michael Jordan in previous contests. He stood at one end of the court and started running. When he got to the opposite free-throw line, Barry took off and soared all the way to the rim. He threw down what became his most memorable jam. He used it again in the finals and was named the winner.

Corey Magette averaged 15.3 points per game in the 2006 playoffs, despite starting only two of the Clippers' 12 postseason games.

PLAYOFF BREAKTHROUGH

By 2006 the Clippers had moved from Buffalo to San Diego to Los Angeles in their three decades of existence. But they had not won a playoff series since 1976.

They didn't have that many chances, of course. The team had reached the postseason only three times in three decades. But when the 2005–06 season began, the Clippers had high hopes. The previous season, they had improved from 28 to 37 victories. The team had a talented young roster featuring power forward Elton Brand, swingman Corey Maggette, and center Chris Kaman. Veteran guards Sam Cassell and Cuttino Mobley arrived that year. The team was ready to get over the hump.

The plan worked. The Clippers won 47 games, their best record since their Buffalo days. They even finished two games ahead of their crosstown rivals, the Lakers. It also earned the Clippers home-court advantage in the first round against the Denver Nuggets. Opening the series in Los Angeles, it was soon clear the Clippers were ready to contend. They held off a late Nuggets rally to win Game 1 89–87. In Game 2, Los Angeles surged to a 22-point halftime lead in a 98–87 victory.

The Nuggets fought back to win Game 3 at home, Los Angeles kept its foot on the gas. In Game 4, seven players scored in double figures in a 100–86 romp. Back in Los Angeles,

Mobley and Maggette each scored 23 as the Clippers clinched their first playoff series victory in 30 years by winning 101–83.

DYNAMIC DUO

Kawhi Leonard and Paul George were brought to Los Angeles to win big games. They delivered on that promise in the first round of the 2021 playoffs. The Clippers needed a rally against the Dallas Mavericks. The Mavericks had upset the Clippers in Los Angeles in the first two games.

After the Clippers battled back in Dallas, the Mavericks won Game 5 105–100. In Game 6, Leonard showed the form that had made him a two-time Finals MVP. He shot 18-for-25, including five three-pointers. Leonard saved his best for the fourth quarter. He was a perfect 5-for-5 from the field. With 3:04 left, the Clippers led 90–88. Leonard took over. He hit a long jump shot and two three-pointers on the next two possessions. Los Angeles held on for a 104–97 win.

Game 7 was back in Los Angeles. But the Clippers had not been using their home-court advantage. They were 0–3 at home in the series. Even worse, Dallas star guard Luka Dončić was lighting up the scoreboard. His 19 first-quarter points gave Dallas a 38–35 lead.

Los Angeles's two stars stepped up again. George scored 13 points in the second quarter. The Clippers trailed 81–79

Kawhi Leonard, *center*, lays in two of his 28 points during Game 7 of Los Angeles's opening round victory over the Dallas Mavericks in the 2021 playoffs.

with 6:09 left in the third quarter. But behind two points from George and seven from Leonard, they went on a 21–4 run.

In the fourth quarter, the Clippers finished off a 126–111 romp. George finished with 22 points and 10 assists. Leonard threatened a triple-double with 28 points, 10 rebounds, and nine assists. More importantly, the duo had delivered playoff success—with the promise of more on the way.

TIMELINE

1970

The NBA expands to 17 teams, adding a new team in Buffalo, New York. The team is called the Braves.

1973

The Braves suffer a third straight losing season, but Bob McAdoo is named NBA Rookie of the Year.

1975

After averaging 34.5 points and 10.3 rebounds per game, McAdoo is named the NBA MVP. He leads the Braves to a second straight playoff appearance, but they lose in the first round.

1976

McAdoo wins his third NBA scoring title in a row, and the Braves finally win a playoff series, defeating the Philadelphia 76ers in the first round.

1978

Boston Celtics owner Irving Levin swaps franchises with the Braves' ownership group. Levin then moves the team to San Diego and renames them the Clippers.

1981

Attorney Donald Sterling purchases the team.

1984

Sterling moves the Clippers to Los Angeles, despite being warned by the NBA not to do so.

1987

The Clippers hit rock bottom, posting a record of 12–70, the worst in the NBA by 12 games.

1992

After winning 45 games—their most since moving to California—the Clippers lose to the Utah Jazz 3–2 in the first round of the playoffs.

1993

The Clippers make their second straight playoff appearance but once again fall in five games during the first round.

1996

Brent Barry wins the NBA Slam Dunk Contest.

1999

Crypto.com Arena, then called Staples Center, opens as the home of both the Clippers and the Lakers.

2006

The Clippers win their first playoff series in 30 years, defeating the Denver Nuggets 4–1.

2011

Blake Griffin becomes the second Clippers rookie to win the NBA Slam Dunk Contest.

2019

Superstar forward Kawhi Leonard signs a free agent contract with the Clippers, who later trade for another star in forward Paul George.

2021

With a six-game victory over the Utah Jazz, the Clippers reach the Western Conference finals for the first time in franchise history.

FACTS

FRANCHISE HISTORY
Buffalo Braves (1970–1978)
San Diego Clippers
  (1978–1984)
Los Angeles Clippers (1984–)

KEY PLAYERS
Elton Brand (2001–08)
Paul George (2019–)
Blake Griffin (2010–18)
DeAndre Jordan (2008–18)
Kawhi Leonard (2019–)
Corey Maggette (2000–08)
Danny Manning (1988–94)
Bob McAdoo (1972–76)
Chris Paul (2011–17)
Randy Smith (1971–79,
  1982–83)
Loy Vaught (1990–98)

KEY COACHES
Mike Dunleavy (2003–10)
Jack Ramsay (1972–76)
Doc Rivers (2013–20)

HOME ARENAS
Buffalo Memorial Auditorium
  (1970–78)
San Diego Sports Arena
  (1978–84)
Los Angeles Memorial Sports
  Arena (1984–99)
Crypto.com Arena (1999–)
  Formerly known as:
  Staples Center (1999–2021)

TRIVIA

CUP OF COFFEE

Hall of Fame center Moses Malone played his first two NBA games with the Buffalo Braves, who promptly traded him to the Houston Rockets in 1976. Other Hall of Famers to briefly play for the Clippers were Jamaal Wilkes (13 games in 1985), Dominique Wilkins (25 games in 1994), and Grant Hill (29 games in 2013).

RECORD COMEBACK

The Clippers' 31-point comeback against the Golden State Warriors in Game 2 of the 2019 Western Conference first round was the biggest comeback in NBA playoffs history.

BIG IN BUFFALO

The Braves played in Buffalo for only eight years, but they had three Rookie of the Year winners in that time. Bob McAdoo won the award in 1973. Point guard Ernie DiGregorio took the honor in 1974. Forward Adrian Dantley was named top rookie in 1977.

CELEBRITY SUITORS

After Donald Sterling was forced to sell the team in 2014, many celebrities were interested in buying the Clippers. While the team was eventually sold to former Microsoft CEO Steve Ballmer, sales to groups that included TV host Oprah Winfrey, boxing champion Floyd Mayweather, and former Los Angeles Lakers star Magic Johnson were all considered.

GLOSSARY

All-American
A player chosen as one of the best amateurs in the country in a particular sport.

alley-oop
A pass that is caught and immediately dunked before the shooter lands on the ground.

assist
A pass that leads directly to a basket.

clipper
A fast sailing ship.

commissioner
The chief executive of a sports league.

contender
A person or team that has a good chance at winning a championship.

draft
A system that allows teams to acquire new players coming into a league.

expansion
The addition of new teams to increase the size of a league.

franchise
A sports organization, including the top-level team and all minor league affiliates.

racist
Prejudiced against a person or group of people based on their background or ethnicity.

rebound
To catch the ball after a shot has been missed.

rookie
A professional athlete in his or her first year of competition.

triple-double
Accumulating 10 or more of three certain statistics in a game.

turnover
Losing the ball to the other team because of a mistake.

MORE **INFORMATION**

BOOKS

Flynn, Brendan. *The NBA Encyclopedia for Kids*. Minneapolis, MN: Abdo Publishing, 2022.

Graves, Will. *NBA*. Minneapolis, MN: Abdo Publishing, 2021.

Mason, Tyler. *Ultimate NBA Road Trip*. Minneapolis, MN: Abdo Publishing, 2019.

ONLINE RESOURCES

To learn more about the Los Angeles Clippers, please visit **abdobooklinks.com** or scan this QR code. These links are routinely monitored and updated to provide the most current information available.

ABOUT THE AUTHOR

Patrick Donnelly is a freelance writer who lives in Minneapolis, Minnesota. He has covered the NBA for 20 years.